Earth Matters
Maps

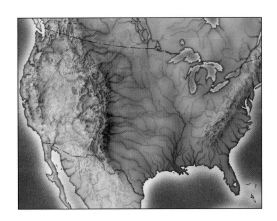

Dana Meachen Rau

Marshall Cavendish
Benchmark
New York

Do you have a new friend coming to visit? How will she know where you live? You can draw a map for her.

Earth is a huge place. People make maps to find places in the world. A *cartographer* is someone who makes maps.

6

Long ago, people did not know what Earth looked like. They had not traveled very far.

People took ships across oceans to new lands. They made maps to remember the way.

A *globe* is a round map of Earth. The large land areas on a globe are *continents*. The large blue areas are oceans.

A map can be flat, too. Flat maps together in a book make an *atlas*.

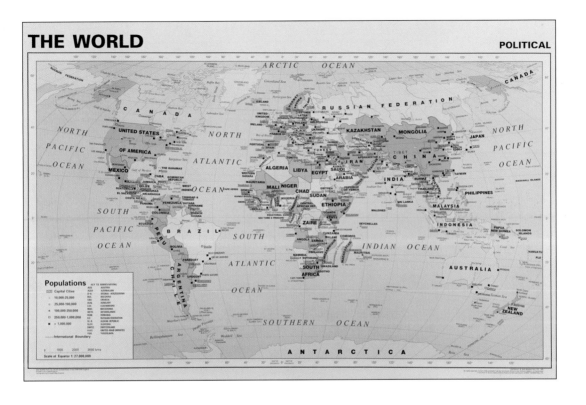

THE WORLD

POLITICAL

Some flat maps show the whole Earth. Other flat maps give you a close view.

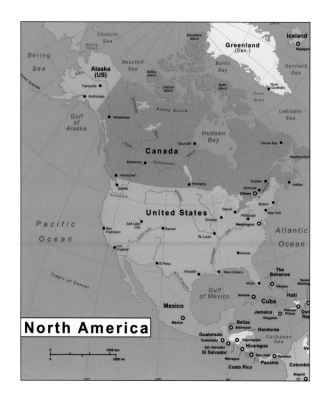

Some maps show you how the land is divided. Continents are divided into countries.

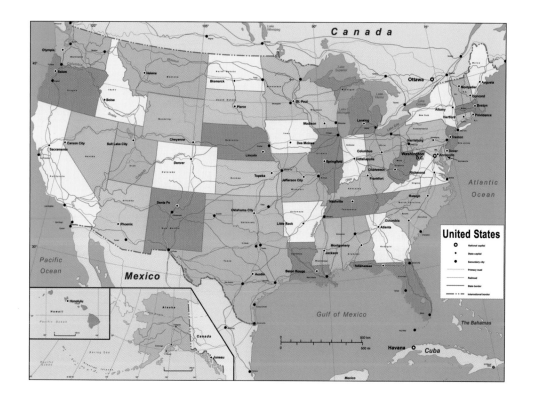

Countries are divided into
states or territories.

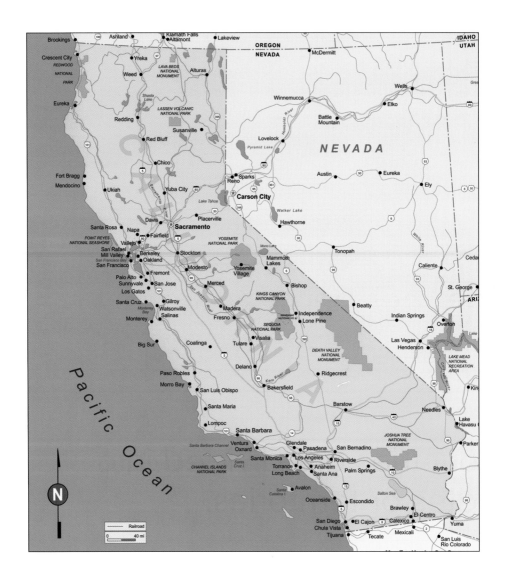

States are divided into *counties*, cities, and towns. The lines between states on a map are called *borders*.

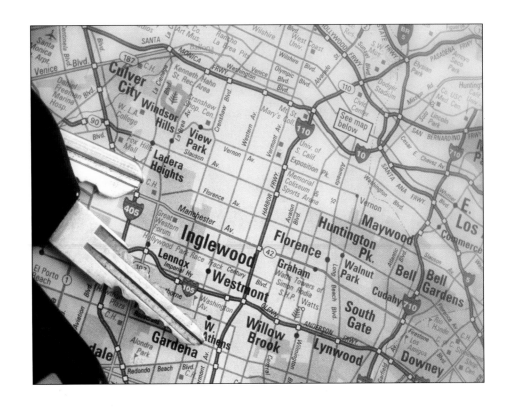

Maps help you go places.
Road maps show the roads in
an area.

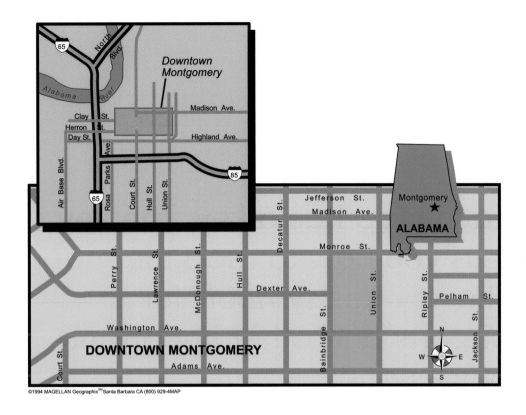

Street maps show the names of streets in a town.

Each map has a *key*. The key tells you how to read the map. The key has *symbols* for airports and other important places.

New York Metro

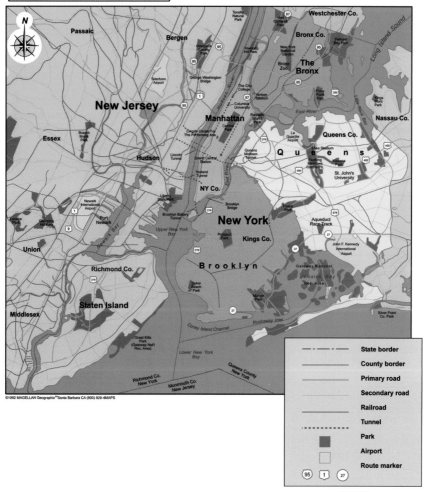

KEY

— · — · — ·	State border
———	County border
———	Primary road
- - - - -	Secondary road
———	Railroad
· ■ ■ ■ ■ ■ ·	Tunnel
■	Park
□	Airport
95 1 27	Route marker

Atlanta

Olympic Sports Venue
Point of Interest
Rail Station

Piedmont Park

Midtown

Georgia Institute of Technology

Marietta Street

W. Peachtree Street

Piedmont Avenue

Coca-Cola Company

North Ave.

North Avenue

Carter Presidential Center

Civic Center

Atlanta Civic Center

Boulevard

Georgia World Congress Center

Highland Avenue

Georgia Dome

Omni Coliseum

Martin Luther King Jr. Historic District

M.L. King Jr. Drive

Omni

Five Points

Georgia State

Clark Atlanta University

Decatur Street

Marta Rail Line

Morehouse College

Garnett

Atlanta City Hall

King Memorial

Oakland Cemetery

Spelman College

Georgia State Capitol

Marta Rail Line

Atlanta-Fulton County Stadium

Grant Park

Boulevard

Georgia Avenue

Zoo Atlanta

Olympic Stadium

Capitol Avenue

0   1/2 mi

N

A key can tell you what different colors on the map mean. It might show the directions north, south, east, and west.

A map also has a *scale*. The scale tells you how big or how far something is on a map. The scale might show 1 inch for 20 miles. If you measure 1 inch from one town to another, that means they are 20 miles apart.

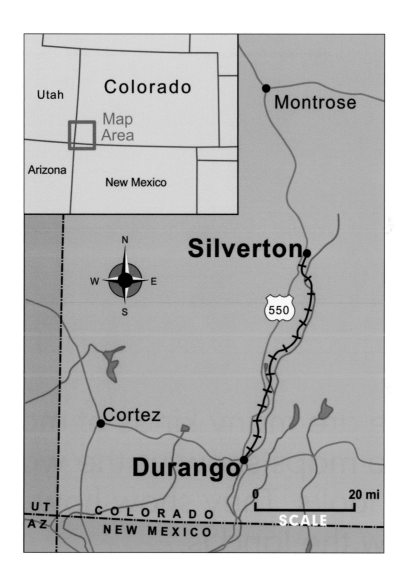

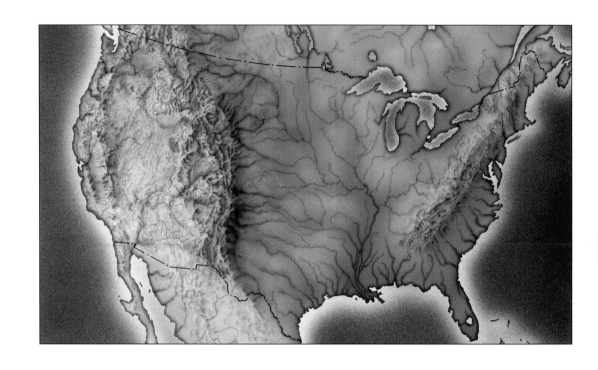

There are many kinds of maps.
Some maps show us the way
land looks. They show how high
or low the land is.

Other maps show landforms
under the ocean.

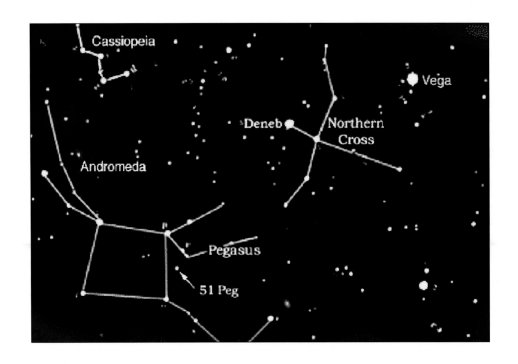

We even have maps of what we can see from Earth. Star maps show what the sky will look like on a certain day.

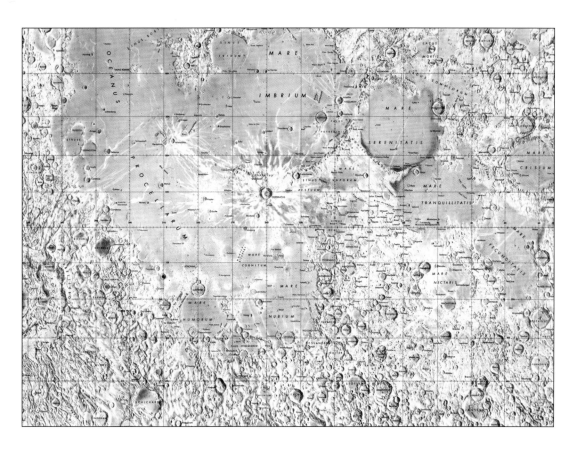

A map of the Moon shows its
many types of land.

Today cartographers do not have to travel the world. They use pictures of Earth taken from space. They make maps to show you where you are in the world.

Challenge Words

atlas (AT-lehs)—Flat maps together in a book.

borders (BOR-dehrs)—The lines on a map between towns, counties, states, or countries.

cartographer (kar-TOG-gruh-fehr)—Someone who makes maps.

continents (KAHN-ti-nehnts)—The seven large land areas on Earth: Asia, Africa, North America, South America, Antarctica, Europe, and Australia.

counties (KOUNT-ees)—One of the areas into which a state is divided.

globe—A round map of Earth.

key (kee)—The part of a map that tells you how to read it.

scale (skale)—The part of a map that helps you figure out distances.

symbols (SIM-buhls)—Small pictures that stand for something else.

Index

Page numbers in **boldface** are illustrations.

With thanks to Nanci Vargus, Ed.D., and Beth Walker Gambro, reading consultants

Marshall Cavendish Benchmark
99 White Plains Road
Tarrytown, New York 10591-5502
www.marshallcavendish.us

Library of Congress Cataloging-in-Publication Data

Rau, Dana Meachen, 1971–
Maps / by Dana Meachen Rau.
p. cm. — (Bookworms. Earth matters)
Summary: "Discusses how people make sense of Earth by making maps and introduces globes, flat maps, and the idea of making borders"—Provided by publisher.
Includes index.
ISBN 978-0-7614-3046-9
1. Maps—Juvenile literature. 2. Cartography—Juvenile literature. I. Title.
GA105.6.R38 2008
912—dc22
2007030283

Editor: Christina Gardeski
Publisher: Michelle Bisson
Designer: Virginia Pope
Art Director: Anahid Hamparian

Photo Research by Anne Burns Images

Cover Photo by *Corbis*/Mike Agliolo

The photographs in this book are used with permission and through the courtesy of:
Corbis: pp. 1, 24 Images.com; p. 5 Roger Ressmeyer; p. 6 Archivo Iconografico; p. 10 Leah Warkentin/Design Pics; pp. 12, 13, 14, 17, 19, 20, 23 Maps.com. *Jupiter Images*: p. 2 Wink; p. 9 Workbook Stock. *Photo Researchers*: p. 11 Map Marketing, Ltd.; p. 25 Mike Agliolo. *Photri/Microstock*: p. 26. *NASA*: p. 27. *Alamy Images*: p. 16 B.A.E. Inc.; p. 29 Trip.

Printed in Malaysia
1   3   5   6   4   2